Backyard **Bugs** &Creepy-Crawlies

# Beetles

**Victoria Hazlehurst**

Explore other books at:
WWW.ENGAGEBOOKS.COM

VANCOUVER, B.C.

e↗ WWW.ENGAGEBOOKS.COM

*Beetles: Level Pre-1*
*Backyard Bugs & Creepy Crawlies*
Roscoe-Roumanis, Victoria 1945 –
Text © 2022 Engage Books
Design © 2022 Engage Books

Edited by: A.R. Roumanis
and Sarah Harvey

Text set in Epilogue

FIRST EDITION / FIRST PRINTING

LIBRARY AND ARCHIVES CANADA CATALOGUING IN PUBLICATION

Title: Beetles / Victoria Roscoe-Roumanis.
Names: Roscoe-Roumanis, Victoria, author.
Description: Series statement: Backyard bugs & creepy-crawlies
Engaging readers: level pre-1, beginner.

Identifiers: Canadiana (print) 20220403473 | Canadiana (ebook) 20220403481
ISBN 978-1-77476-716-0 (hardcover)
ISBN 978-1-77476-717-7 (softcover)
ISBN 978-1-77476-718-4 (epub)
ISBN 978-1-77476-719-1 (pdf)

Subjects:
LCSH: Beetles—Juvenile literature.

Classification: LCC QL576.2 .R68 2022 | DDC J595.76—DC23

This project has been made possible in part by the Government of Canada.

Canada

# My real name is lady beetle!

Beetles are insects.
They can live almost
anywhere on Earth.

Beetles like to be in the ground or inside trees.

Adult beetles have six legs and two sets of wings.

**Crimean Ground Beetle**

**Legs**

Hard outer wings protect the lighter inner wings.

Outer Wings

# Some beetles are very noisy.

June Beetle

Bark beetles chirp.
June beetles squeal.

Beetles can be almost any color.

Dogbane Beetle

They may have
spots or stripes.

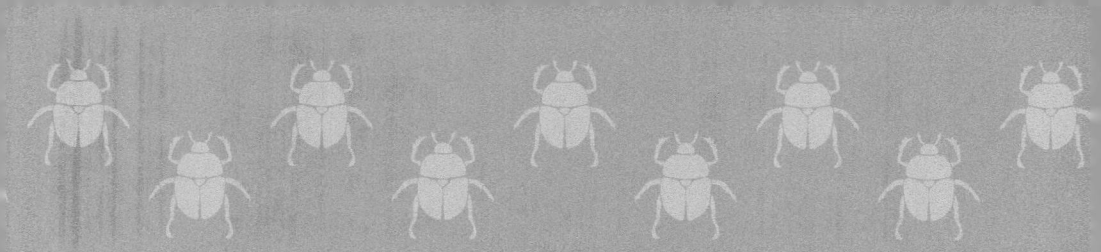

The titan beetle is the largest beetle in the world.

It lives in the forests of South America.

15

The firefly is a kind of beetle.

It glows yellow or green at night.

The tiger beetle is
the fastest insect
in the world.

It can cross a football field in 43 seconds.

19

A female beetle can lay many eggs at a time.

Potato Beetle

The eggs turn into grubs. Grubs become cocoons.

Beetles hatch
from cocoons.

Some beetles destroy gardens, trees, and wood.

Other beetles spread pollen from flower to flower.

Spreading pollen helps plants grow new seeds.

Aphid

I eat aphids that are hurting plants!

# Explore other books in the Backyard Bugs & Creepy Crawlies series!

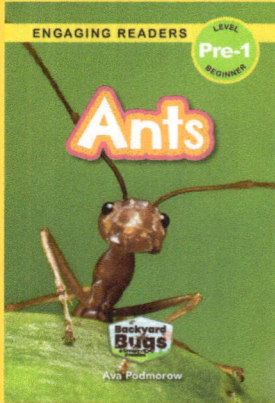

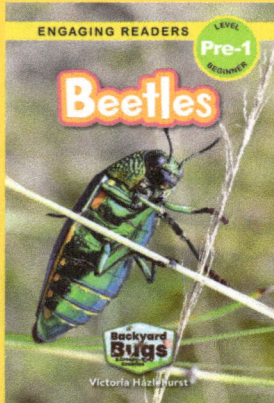

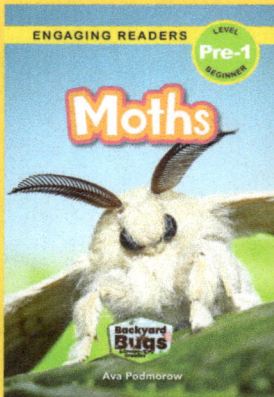

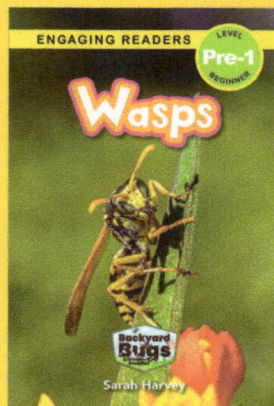

Visit www.engagebooks.com/readers

# Explore books in the Animals In The City series.

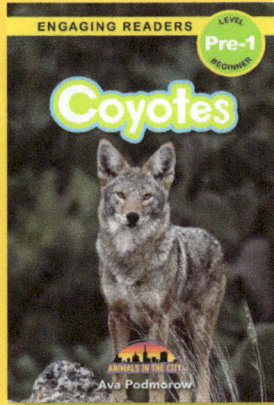

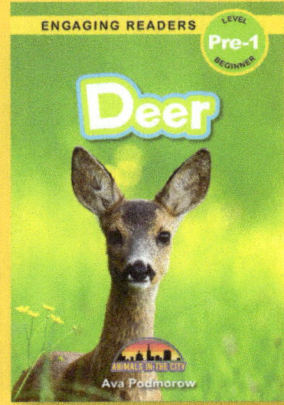

ENGAGING READERS — Pre-1 — LEVEL BEGINNER
**Cats**
ANIMALS IN THE CITY
Ava Podmorow

ENGAGING READERS — Pre-1 — LEVEL BEGINNER
**Coyotes**
ANIMALS IN THE CITY
Ava Podmorow

ENGAGING READERS — Pre-1 — LEVEL BEGINNER
**Deer**
ANIMALS IN THE CITY
Ava Podmorow

ENGAGING READERS — Pre-1 — LEVEL BEGINNER
**Owls**
ANIMALS IN THE CITY
Ava Podmorow

ENGAGING READERS — Pre-1 — LEVEL BEGINNER
**Pigeons**
ANIMALS IN THE CITY
Ava Podmorow

ENGAGING READERS — Pre-1 — LEVEL BEGINNER
**Rabbits**
ANIMALS IN THE CITY
Ava Podmorow

ENGAGING READERS — Pre-1 — LEVEL BEGINNER
**Raccoons**
ANIMALS IN THE CITY
Sarah Harvey

ENGAGING READERS — Pre-1 — LEVEL BEGINNER
**Rats**
ANIMALS IN THE CITY
Ava Podmorow

ENGAGING READERS — Pre-1 — LEVEL BEGINNER
**Skunks**
ANIMALS IN THE CITY
Ava Podmorow

Visit www.engagebooks.com/readers

www.ingramcontent.com/pod-product-compliance
Lightning Source LLC
Chambersburg PA
CBHW051235020426

42331CB00016B/3380